Sara's Surprise

Written by Marie Gibson

Illustrated by Margaret Power

Sara lived in an apartment
on the third floor.
She wanted to have a garden.

3

"Gary has a garden. He grows
carrots in his garden," Sara said.
"He had a carrot for lunch today."

5

"We can't have a garden,"
Mom said. "But you can grow
something in a pot."

Sara and Mom went to the plant store. Mom got a big pot and a bag of soil. Sara chose the seeds.

"What seeds did you get?" Mom asked.

"It's a surprise," Sara said.

Sara filled the pot with soil.
She put it by the window
and planted her seeds.

After a while, some green shoots came up.

"What are they?" Mom asked.

"It's a surprise," Sara said.

Sara watered the seeds,
and soon there were
lots of green leaves.
She picked some.

"Wait for the flowers," Mom said.

"I'm not growing flowers," Sara said.

"It's lettuce," Sara said.
"I'm making a salad.
Do you want some?"